The Following Scan
Will Last Five Minutes

The Following Scan Will Last Five Minutes

Lieke Marsman

translated by

Sophie Collins

English edition first published 2019 by
Liverpool University Press
4 Cambridge Street
Liverpool
L69 7ZU

English translation copyright and text copyright of
Translator's Note: Dear Lieke © 2019 Sophie Collins
Text copyright © 2018 Lieke Marsman
Originally published by Uitgeverij Pluim, Amsterdam | Antwerp
under the title *De volgende scan duurt vijf minuten*

British Library Cataloguing-in-Publication data
A British Library CIP record is available

ISBN 978-1-78694-213-5 softback

Typeset by Carnegie Book Production, Lancaster
Printed and bound in Poland by Booksfactory.co.uk

✦ ✦ ✦ ✦ ✦

Every once in a while I would think, 'what do I eat? how do I act to announce or preserve my new status as temporary upon this earth?' and then I'd remember that we have always been temporary, and that I had just never really underlined it before, or acted out of it so completely before. And then I would feel a little foolish and needlessly melodramatic, but only a little.

– Audre Lorde, *The Cancer Journals*

The Following Scan
Will Last Four Minutes

Before you sink away
into the morphinesweet unreality of the everyday
we would like to say something
about those spasms and fasciculations of yours
as well as that bump on your back

For years you have no doubt
been googling every freckle. Just recently
you were at the doctor's with a patch
of dry skin on your leg
Diagnosis: too much shower gel
But on hearing the word *chondrosarcoma*
you went home and immediately unplugged your router
Do you know where your priorities lie?

Do you know what life has to offer
or did those endless therapy sessions
and that eight-week mindfulness course
simply teach you how to tolerate suffering
that every signal in your body
can be temporarily expelled
to the rhythm of some breathing exercise?
> *Let the pain be*
> *To be free is to be free of need*
Wrong
To be free is to need some fresh air
and to be able to get up and go outside

Don't say we didn't warn you

Identity Politics Are a Fad, You Say

And I say, Fads are our political identity
Manifestations of our political choices
deeply rooted in who we are
fads and trends are the gateways
the last available lifeboats
in the artificial wave pool of our image-centred age

And I am just so scared of disappearing
that I am prepared to grasp onto anything
Is there a hacktivist
who could interrupt mortality?

Is there a way
to let out a single scream
without anyone feeling the need to respond, while
at the same time making it known
that I desperately need to hear
from other sufferers?

We are all sufferers, you say,
and we already hear far too much from one another

Treats

Irrationality
is an emergent property
that cannot be explained
in terms of the brain's
cellular processes, but
can nonetheless be proven
to exist, as in instances
of love or of sickness
when we believe we will die,
but do not die,

not yet. Evolution
is a kind of by-product:
positive development
occurs in one small area
while everything else
is razed. How does luck
figure in these terms? Life
gives you fun-size packs of Croky
and your heart beats faster
as it registers the treat. With any luck
there'll be a few paprika left
(your favourite). But tell me why
some of us collide with trees
at well-lit junctions, while others
swerve cliff edges in deep fog?
You can make your own good luck, it's true,
but that won't preclude the bad.

We torture mice, engineer
heart disease in monkeys, burn
pigs alive. The white rhino

is dying out. How unfortunate to be the last
white rhino. Or how lucky? Panic
feels like butterflies flitting chaotically
around the buckthorn, knowing
they've got just twenty-four hours
to live. Only heat can soothe me. Not
the swampy warmth of the polders,
but the dry kind
that determines the diaspora
of Dutch holiday-makers. Still each day
feels like a choice between vitamin D
deficiency and skin cancer.
Even in Tuscany.

Not long ago, under the heat of a sun so dry
the bark began to fall away from the trees,
I thought of Wittgenstein's
Tractatus and *Investigations*.
Could cries of fear
be the only language games
that are universally
understood? Along with, perhaps,
the anticipation of the treat?
Somewhere, a hatch snaps open.
A mouse gets a piece of banana. Tiny squeaks
escape my lungs
when I am most afraid.
Whereof one cannot speak,
thereof one forms silent gestures
or bursts into tears.

The Following Scan
Will Last Two Minutes

It is 1952
Bright colours exist only in nature
do not yet fill the aisles of Xenos
You can add an egg to the cake mix
to make yourself feel like a good housewife
Somewhere on the outskirts of Twente
my great-grandfather is dying of bladder cancer

It is 2018
You can separate glass from paper
to make yourself feel like a good citizen
You use a linen shopping bag
You give readings about the environment
You travel off-peak using a discount
You no longer have the strength to collect the small change
you get for recycling bottles at the supermarket
You just throw them all in the general waste

The Following Scan
Will Last Less Than a Minute

all over the country
upscale housing developments metastase
their windows filled with ceramic vases
containing dried reeds, lilies
Buddha oversees it all, serene
but what dangers is he protecting against?
there is no danger
no one here is on benefits
everyone is at work
no one sees the rain
making rings in the ponds
with fountains
and koi carp
except perhaps the woman on the red mobility scooter
riding over paving stones, pink superellipses
like sandwich meat

The Following Scan
Will Last Less Than a Minute

afternoons are
Eurosport replays
of alpine skiing
sponsored by Jack Wolfskin and Milka
brands to whom I am grateful
for facilitating this daily moment of calm

evenings are the joy
I take in loving Simone as much as I do
especially in the face of this overwhelming exhaustion

cancer is so quotidian
you hear about it on Wednesday morning
die on a Tuesday afternoon
no strobe lights
no cloakroom check-in
the sun is shining
a completely ordinary insipid sun
above the A10
and the exit for Praxis

The Following Scan
Will Last Three Minutes

God, grant us the confidence
of a mediocre white man
my girlfriends pray
at modern-day séances
with candles
trading knowledge
and wine
People call my girlfriends hysterical
tell them to keep calm
while men initiate price wars
or regular wars
the kind involving weapons

The Following Scan
Will Last Three Minutes

While cycling through the city I pick up now and then
the unmistakeable scent of pork schnitzel
and beurre blanc, Trappist beer
and Iberico ham, aromatic sensations
that set me back on the right path
leading me deeper into Europe
Personally I've been a believer in multiculturalism
since the popularisation of the kebab, still
I've felt gloomy on occasion
because which of the nineties' promises
have actually come to pass
save the unmitigated rise of reality TV, where
a number of major developments
have indeed been recorded?

That you can say anything you like
doesn't mean
that you should say anything
If I were to give you a beautiful piece of land
with which you could do anything you like
I doubt you'd go and shit all over it

In truth though it's the unsaid
that determines who gets promoted
and who gets deported
There is a violence in the inertia of politicians
Their endless deferrals effect real violence

The Following Scan
Will Last One Minute

with cancer in your back everything
is suddenly afforded an epic quality

two people in a car
magical!

tying your own shoelaces
the stuff of poetry!

Simone feeding me recovery ward noodles
a fairy tale

The Following Scan
Will Last Five Minutes

The internet has a great deal to offer
Someone who doesn't wish to dwell
For whom every breath is a distraction

Throbbing lung tumours
The man in the street
Is always right

The nation state has been disarticulated
By her opponents
Then glorified

By her supporters
The man in the street
Is always right

The news repeats itself
The rhythm of drones
The oncologist commences sentencing

There is nothing I need to see
Except, again and again,
A new day with you

The MRI tunnel speaks
The following scan will last five minutes
Poetry fills this empty head

Contrast agent
The stench of anaesthetic
A beach ball in your nose

A volleyball in your stomach
Poetry fills this empty head
The rhythm falters

The news repeats itself
Language without sound
Cancer without catharsis

There is nothing I need to see
Except, again and again,
A new day

How Are You Feeling?

1.

I had already inserted myself into the narrative of an overworked twenty-something-year-old. Successful career, hectic social life, high ambitions – aren't these the signs of an impending burn-out? I was also experiencing some mild pain in my right shoulder due to a repetitive strain injury. The physiotherapist to whom I was referred by my GP wasn't the least alarmed. Perhaps I should get a new office chair or set an egg-timer to ensure that I take regular breaks from working, she suggested. A few months later, I discovered the blade of the shoulder in question was slightly raised. The pain had not lessened. December came around and I upgraded to a health insurance plan with better coverage for continued physiotherapy. I found a new physio and practised the set exercises until I was blue in the face, but there was little to no improvement. I went back to the GP, who pointed me towards orthopaedics and gave me my first diagnosis: neuralgic amyotrophy, a rare disorder in which the muscles supporting the shoulder blade start to degenerate. The orthopaedist went along with this (it later became clear that he hadn't properly examined the X-rays, or hadn't examined them at all) and referred me to a neurologist. Further tests were necessary, said the neurologist, but mine was not an urgent case. The waiting list for an MRI scan was about two months long, and I should prepare myself for the likelihood that nothing would be found.

In the month that follows the pain develops into a chronic nerve pain, the sort of pain that pulls you from sleep and sucks away joy. I'm about to head to the town of Tilburg for a week, having been appointed writer-in-residence for the local literary festival. I'm not sure what to do. I don't feel good about cancelling a commitment I made almost a year ago with the words 'Sorry, my shoulder hurts', especially now I know there's nothing to be too concerned about. I decide to go to Tilburg. Once there, however, I end up lying in bed for most of the day, managing to crawl out now and then in order to give a performance or be photographed for the local newspaper. On the day of the festival I put my back out and am only able to perform sitting down. What the hell am I doing, I ask myself as I finally ease into a hot bath at one in the morning. I feel as though all the energy has left my body. Finally, I'm certain: this is what they mean when they say 'burn-out'.

—

Two days after returning from Tilburg I finally have my MRI scan; it's been brought forward by a month because the pain has become unbearable. My girlfriend Simone phoned the hospital to ask whether they could possibly see me any earlier. It's been a long time since I've felt able to assert myself, I'm just so tired. I've been told repeatedly that I'll have to wait and I don't have the strength to protest. I'm still not sure how Simone did it, but, after a few phone calls from her, the appointment was rescheduled.

The scan seems to last for hours. The MRI tunnel announces and reannounces subsequent scans. The following scan will last five minutes, the following scan will last four minutes, the following scan will last one minute, the following scan will last five minutes.

—

The following morning I wake up early with a sense of anticipation: it's the morning of the local elections. Election days are my favourite days of the year. For a moment I allow myself to remember the House of Representatives elections from the previous year, how I had walked, full of hope (and even a little teary), to the primary school around the corner to cast my vote (it's fair to say that I'm a bit of an emotional wreck on such days).

I pick up my phone to check the latest poll forecasts as I put my voting card into my bag. It's at that moment that I notice the hospital have called and left a message on my voicemail. They want me to go in. Because the hospital isn't more than fifty metres from my front door (I live right in the city centre) and because I suspect they're calling as they've finally decided to give me the painkillers I've begged for several times over the phone, I decide to go straight there. Fifteen minutes later, I walk into the neurology department. The neurologist looks nervous as he opens the images from the scan. No one expected this, he says, but there's a tumour. It's big. And it's malignant.

—

It's a scene that I'll replay in my mind again and again over the coming months. Cancer of the cartilage. A malignant tumour in my upper back, 8 × 9 × 10 centimetres in size. So well-hidden behind my right shoulder blade that two physios, three replacement physios, a GP, an orthopaedist, a radiologist and the neurologist currently sitting opposite me were able to miss it. The diagnosis is a surprise to everyone.

—

I call my parents. I call Simone. They make their way to me as quickly as they can. I am in a complete daze, resting my head on the neurologist's desk, its surface cold against my cheek.

A PA (physician associate) is explaining what will happen next. They are unable to deal with the tumour at this hospital, so they've made me an appointment for the following day in the AMC (Amsterdam Medical Centre), a hospital affiliated with the University of Amsterdam. The tumour is no longer self-contained. It has colonised a large area of muscle. This is no good sign. But they are unable to give me any further information about treatment and prognosis. Am I going to die? They have no idea. The neurologist scrolls once more through the images from the MRI scan. They show a big white ball containing lots of other, smaller white balls. It reminds me of a cauliflower. I'm unable to sit up fully, which could either be due to the tumour or to the shock – I'm not sure which.

What now? I have no clue what now. I should go vote, I think. I need to go vote. But first I go to the pub on the corner and order a double whiskey. That it's eleven in the morning makes no difference to me.

—

In the AMC I learn that chondrosarcoma or cancer of the cartilage is a rare type that typically affects older people. It's also a strange kind in that it doesn't react to chemotherapy or radiotherapy. The only way to treat it is to remove as much of it as possible. Luckily, the prognosis for this approach is relatively good. Unless the cancer has spread. Then it'll be another story. So I need to have a PET-CT scan right away.

—

As I slide into the PET-CT scanner a few days later, I have an epiphany. If I survive this, I'm never going to do underpaid work ever again. Never again will I perform for the Rotary Club of this or that provincial town, never again will I give poetry lessons to teenagers. As a writer, I'm probably supposed to enjoy these things. But I do not enjoy these things. Maybe, just maybe, I'll never do anything that makes me unhappy ever again.

—

Another few days after the scan, I have the operation. The tumour and affected tissue are painstakingly cut away and removed. Unfortunately, my shoulder blade and a large amount of muscle end up in the bin too. But my arm is still attached. And, most importantly, the PET-CT scan didn't detect any metastasis. Somewhere far away, someone says my name. I slowly wake from a seven-hour, dreamless sleep. I feel pretty sexy in my light blue hospital gown; it's a colour I've always thought gives my skin the look of a subtle tan. In reality, Simone later tells me, I looked more or less green.

—

In the recovery ward, I feel – strangely – entirely at home. It's the only logical outcome of the previous year, a sign that my complaints have finally been taken seriously. The operation was a success, and I'm now lying with a series of tubes in my arms in a hospital room with a view of the A10.

I find myself thinking about the past. Not of one particular memory from childhood, but in the sense that I feel like a child again. A child mentally drained from a day at school, powerless but carefree, because someone else is responsible for me, will look after me. To stay inside that feeling I listen to the music I was listening to when I was ten: K-otic, Westlife (yes, really), the soundtrack from *Annie*. But I soon feel the kind of sadness that only a child can feel, a sadness that's a hard longing for the world, for everything. A sadness that tells you that so much is happening beyond the edges of your small town – but what is it? When will someone finally take it upon themselves to tell you what's waiting for you, for the rest of your life? And how the hell have you ended up in this hospital? Luckily I'm hooked up to a morphine drip that allows me to administer the drug to myself at the push of a button. *The sun'll come out tomorrow, bet your bottom dollar that tomorrow, there'll be sun ...*

—

Six days later, I'm allowed to go home. 'Patient was able to leave hospital in good condition', it says in my discharge summary, which effectively means 'patient was able to climb out of bed unsupported and no longer cries when hoisted onto ward's mobile toilet'. But patient has never been so thankful.

2.

In the weeks following my hospitalisation I read *The Cancer Journals* by Audre Lorde and *Illness as Metaphor* by Susan Sontag. *The Cancer Journals* is a personal and at times emotional account of Lorde's experience of breast cancer. *Illness as Metaphor* is an exceedingly rational book in which Sontag, who also suffered from breast cancer, discusses the social status of cancer and cancer patients, focusing mainly on the influence of language and metaphor on our perception of certain diseases. The difference in the tone and approach of these two books is huge, and it gets me thinking. How will I relate to my own disease? Is this a choice? I know it's too early for me to address my situation rationally; I can't move my arm again yet and my first control scans are just around the corner. I find myself bursting into tears at the tiniest things, as when I'm unable to find the nail clippers or a matching sock. And also whenever someone asks me how I'm feeling.

Both Lorde's and Sontag's books are attempts to challenge the taboo surrounding cancer. Sontag deconstructs the mystifying language that surrounded cancer in the seventies (the Big C, the Long Illness), while Lorde writes as openly and honestly as possible about her breast cancer and mastectomy. Today, writing about cancer is more or less destigmatised. Cancer is everywhere – it's the subject of TV shows and books, of countless sponsored walks and runs. Still I notice that my disease makes some people uncomfortable; some of my friends turn into guardian angels, doing my shopping or sending me a postcard every day or bringing me Swedish puzzle books, while others seem to disappear.

In *AIDS and Its Metaphors*, a later book, Sontag writes, 'Twelve years ago, when I became a cancer patient, what particularly enraged me – and distracted me from my own terror and despair at my doctors' gloomy prognosis – was seeing how much the very reputation of this illness added to the suffering of those who have it.' This is a statement that is still completely relevant. For the time being, I've been in a less life-threatening situation than someone with advanced pneumonia, but cancer is a game of chance, and relying on chance makes people nervous. Twenty-seven-year-old bodies are not supposed to get sick, and if they do get sick, it should be due to some tropical disease contracted while traveling the world. Am I experiencing this cancer as an Actual Hell because that's how I genuinely feel about it, or because that is the common perception of cancer, particularly for those who get it at a young age?

—

There are a few reasons the poems in this little book are about cancer and politics, and not just about cancer. Firstly, I had to write about politics in order not to be totally subsumed by the cancer. Continuing to preoccupy myself with the things I was engaged with before the diagnosis helps with my recovery. No matter how much support you get from those around you, cancer is, like every other disease, a very lonely experience. It hurls you into yourself. To be petrified of your own death has to be the loneliest experience there is. It's a loneliness I experienced as unbearable, but one that was in some ways easy to shake off by practicing social criticism.

—

Another reason is that I probably wouldn't have watched the entire dividend tax enquiry of April 25th 2018 had I not been at home sick on the sofa. In a state of disbelief I witnessed how the Dutch administration, under the leadership of our prime minister, Mark Rutte, and the Minister of Economic Affairs, Eric Wiebes, was shown to have made the decision to grant 1.4 billion euros to multinationals like Shell and Unilever each and every year without a single acceptable explanation. The sole 'research-based' basis for such a decision, dredged up from ancient departmental memos, was approximately ten-years-old, and, it transpired, came from a report that had been commissioned by Shell themselves. I've always found it incomprehensible that a coalition government that claims to stand for the principles of a free market in fact affords multinationals like Shell all kinds of tax benefits, but what I was witnessing here represented a whole new level of hypocrisy.

—

Yet another reason: as your perception of your own position in relation to your birth and death becomes suddenly clearer, so too does your perception of your position in relation to the rest of society. For years I've been echoing the opinion that nurses should receive higher salaries, but I had never seen with my own eyes just how hard nurses work. For years I've been echoing the opinion that the pharmaceutical industry is rotten to the core, but I had never stood in a pharmacy with a receipt in my hand for a medicine that's no longer available. Being sick turns the world upside down, and in the chaos that arises abstract policy decisions reveal themselves to be, in practice, fundamental in determining whether the hospital ward you're lying in is understaffed or not. Decisions pertaining to health care are not economic decisions, but decisions about life and death. And with a drip in your hand and twenty stitches in your back it's difficult to believe that the Dutch government have, for decades, opted to cut back on life. You do not cut back on life. Not if you can afford to spare 1.4 billion euros a year.

—

'Any one of us might run into bad luck,' said the parliamentary leader for the VVD[1] Klaas Dijkhoff one month later, at the party's annual conference. And with that he proposed to reduce benefits. 'Because then we can establish a system that is not only inimical to instances of bad luck, but in which each and every person in our society must do his or her best to get back on their own two feet as soon as possible should they encounter it.' Listening to this, I was aware that I hadn't had any income for a couple of months, that I had just looked up how to claim disability benefits, which were indeed available to me on the condition that I change my current status from 'self-employed' to 'unemployed' and forfeit the little bit of money I had already paid into my pension. No problem, I thought; my pension was looking further away than ever at this point.

Bad luck. I've thought about the expression a lot. It sounds inconvenient, but not too terrible. We all encounter it – of course that's correct. But would an everyday instance of bad luck really lead to a situation in which you're no longer able to work at all and are therefore forced to claim disability benefits? Someone like Dijkhoff might have a vault of savings or a wealthy uncle to lean on, but we can't all be so lucky.

---

[1] In the Netherlands, the VVD (Volkspartij voor Vrijheid en Democratie or, in English, People's Party for Freedom and Democracy) has been the largest party for years. Nominally speaking, they are conservative liberal, but in practice they have revealed themselves to be neoliberal, presenting as a right-leaning, albeit more 'sophisticated' alternative to the PVV's (Partij voor de Vrijheid or Party for Freedom's) far-right policies. Over the years, however, the VVD have become increasingly populist and anti-immigration. They are also the party with the highest amount of fraud-based legal cases on their hands. Their current party slogan is 'Doe. Normaal.' or 'Act. Normal.' – something like the English 'Keep Calm and Carry On', this is a play on the Dutch expression 'Doe normaal!'.

'Bad luck', by its very definition, indicates a situation that is a) a one-off, unique and b) accidental. But bad luck can have a knock-on effect, with one instance leading directly to another, which can then lead to another, etc., etc. – in which case, even the accidental does not, as Dijkhoff suggests, have a fixed and temporary timeframe, and so the situation is no longer a mere question of 'bad luck'. You might call a cancer diagnosis a run-in with 'bad luck', but the fallout of that diagnosis (going into long-term treatment, post-traumatic stress, the loss of a limb, breast or job) is most definitely not.

Another form of 'bad luck' is being born at the wrong time, in the wrong place. In a disadvantaged area, for example, or to parents who harm you or have substance abuse issues. The damaging effects this wreaks on your wellbeing for the rest of your life is no case of 'bad luck', but a consequence of the way our society deals with those who are less fortunate – not uniquely, not accidentally. Time and again studies have shown that growing up in poverty affects the trajectory of an individual's entire life. Those who grow up in poverty have a lower life expectancy, are more prone to illness, psychological disorders, lack skills and education, etc. And they account for the majority of those claiming disability benefits.

In other words, being forced to claim disability benefits has nothing to do with bad luck at all. Bad luck is when you are on your way to work and step in dogshit. Really bad luck is when the same thing happens the following day. The reasons that people claim disability benefits are the result of systematic failures of the neoliberal society in which we live, itself neither temporary nor accidental. To deny this is a misunderstanding and an insult to everyone who has ever had to deal with a chronic illness or poverty, or both.

—

At the moments when I fear the cancer has returned, the simplest action becomes a colossal task. Even if I were to physically pass most medical exams, rest assured that, on the days when I am waiting for scan results, I would not tick any of the required boxes, am unable to do the laundry, to even ball my socks. My working memory is completely spent on anticipating that phone call that's still seventy-two hours away, seventy-one hours, seventy, sixty-nine ...

—

How much of an individual's working memory is swallowed up by the experience of fleeing a warzone? Imagine that you are forced to leave your home – immediately – because bombs are being dropped around you, or because your country's government has threatened to execute you and/or abduct your children. The journey that follows is interminable, exhausting. You lose family members and friends along the way. Now imagine that once you arrive in a safer place, you must straight away and under enormous pressure learn a new language, which means not only getting to grips with new words, but learning to read text backwards. And that's if you can already read. If you can't complete this task, it's possible you'll be sent back to the place you were forced to leave. In any case, you'll be given a considerable fine.[2] Oh well, we all run into bad luck.

—

---

[2] In the Netherlands, asylum seekers must complete their inburgerings-examen or citizenship exams, which contain questions such as 'What is an acceptable way of celebrating your birthday with your co-workers?' Another part of the exams is a language skills test. If you fail this test, there are financial consequences.

That speech of Dijkhoff's is an example of the most sickening kind of populism there is: the people in the room full of VVD members will probably never have to think about claiming benefits themselves. The measures they take will likely never become part of reality (after all, it would cost far more for the government to put this law into practice than the law itself would end up profiting them), and so a statement like Dijkhoff's is invoked purely for incitement, to cause unrest among those who – unlike the political class – are already short of money. So what am I so concerned about if it looks like the cutbacks aren't going to be implemented, at least for the time being? I am concerned about the fact that there are people with so little empathy that they respond to the announcement of such policies with cheers. I am concerned that these people interpret their myopic view of the world, their solipsism, as nothing more than confirmation that everything is more or less well in the world. The fact is that the VVD party slogan 'Doe. Normaal.' is taken up by these people as a guise through which they feel able to voice the most antisocial proposals. If someone tells you how calm they are in a super loud voice, you can be sure they're about to say something controversial, or to attempt to normalise an absurd idea.

—

The loneliness of the cancer patient can be temporarily relieved through contact with other sufferers. But cancer patients desire contact with other sufferers mainly when they are at their worst. Because of this, cancer's image can seem, to each sufferer, to always be accompanied by endless battles and recurrent tumours or other bad news. One of the benefits of contact with other patients is that it is free and cannot be suddenly taken away by government cutbacks, in contrast with the specialised psych-oncological care of Mark Rutte's first cabinet. One consultation with one psychologist specialising in cancer will now cost a patient without the correct DSM-5 label[3] ninety-eight euros.

—

The day after writing the above, I see prime minister Rutte in a 'Sta op tegen kanker' or 'Stand Up to Cancer' advert.

---

3   DSM is an acronym for the *Diagnostic and Statistical Manual of Mental Disorders*. As its title suggests, this is a diagnostic manual used by health insurance companies to decide which treatments they will cover and which they will not. In the Netherlands, these companies previously covered most mental illnesses, but, because of Mark Rutte's first cabinet, treatment for cancer-related mental issues (or other life-changing events for that matter) are no longer covered. There are loopholes. For example, a psychologist could refer you specifically for post-traumatic stress disorder or depression. Ultimately, however, the signal the Dutch government is giving is clear: cancer patients shouldn't require psychological help.

3.

Have I thought too often about which songs I would like played at my funeral? Should I have engaged less in Twitter feuds? Are my jokes a little on the mean side? I am seized, now and then, by a deep, old feeling of guilt. Waiting for the results of a scan feels like waiting for sentencing. Only the oncologist is the judge and you're sure you've done nothing wrong. Or maybe you did do something wrong? Did you put enough pressure on the doctors to examine you as quickly and as thoroughly as possible? Did you have too much fun as a student, or perhaps not enough? Are *you*, my reader, getting enough enjoyment from *your* life?

—

Sometimes I refer to my tumour lovingly as my grapefruit, while on other days I vehemently detest it and fantasise about breaking into the tissue bank where it is being stored, in strips, in minus eighty degrees centigrade. At night I dream about wandering along the research centre's corridors, storage cases flipping open left and right, revealing the most gruesome flesh monsters.

—

On more than one occasion I have heard people say that you shouldn't use the expression 'fight against cancer' because this implies that those who died of the disease did not fight it hard enough. That a patient has influence over the outcome of their illness, in other words. But what else am I supposed to tell myself when I wake up in the morning? 'Come on then, time to passively undergo everything that comes your way, just sit back and wait to see what the doctors and more importantly fate have in store for you'?

I *need* the illusion that I can influence my illness and recovery process, and so I tell myself that this is a fight. Is this unfair to those who did not survive the battle with cancer? No. What is unfair for those who died of cancer is the fact that there are others who have never been sick and yet feel they have the right to tell cancer patients how to talk about their own illness. The hardest fighting happens in the wars where there are no winners. That goes for cancer too. If the battle metaphor works for you, use it and know that you may win or lose.

—

In the endless streams of waiting rooms I visit, I read an endless stream of glossy magazines. In every one of these glossy magazines is an article about the effects of stress on the body. We live in a culture that tells us that any psychological issues we might experience are the products of our own minds, because serious research into physical symptoms leads to elevated treatment costs. Meditation and mindfulness are helpful in terms of alleviating pain and fatigue, but where does the pain and fatigue come from in the first place? Dutch healthcare is at an exceptionally high level, but my experience is that it is still very difficult to go to a doctor or to a hospital and be taken seriously. Many of the relaxation techniques that I read about while waiting might be brilliant in theory, but in practice they are the last resort of those with untreated symptoms.

And if there are in fact physical symptoms that are the direct result of stress alone, the following still applies: prevention is better than (temporary) relief. What prevents stress is removing its cause, not weekend supplement after weekend supplement, glossy magazine after glossy magazine describing how stress manifests, who gets stressed and – important! – which products or treatments you can buy in order to reduce stress. The causes of stress in young people, for example, aren't too little Ashtanga Yoga or a lack of fitness boot camps, but zero-hour contracts, increasing student debts and a stagnating housing market. Personally, I'd like to see more lifestyle section pieces on these issues.

—

Lorde: 'We live in a profit economy and there is no profit in the prevention of cancer; there is only profit in the treatment of cancer.'

—

The importance of informal social care or family care cannot be stressed enough; in some cases, it is absolutely the best way for someone to receive care. But what must also be stressed is the fact that, in most cases, this kind of dedicated care is a last resort. When politicians say that they endorse so-called informal carers, what they are actually saying is that they endorse unpaid labour. Informal care and home care are two very different things that should not be confused. Surely it's a nice thing to be cared for by someone you know? Personally I found it an excellent way to make hitherto equal relationships unequal. I do not want my girlfriend, who I had only known for a few months when I first became ill, to dress my wounds. I don't want to be washed by the person who sleeps next to me at night. I was so happy when, at twenty-seven, I finally felt able to stand on my own two feet, to not have to constantly call my parents for their help with this or that.

—

Sometimes I worry that cancer has made me egotistical. Someone says something to me and I don't hear the words. I'm just sitting there thinking, 'How soon is too soon to start talking about cancer?' I want to tell my story again. And again. When I'm conversing with myself about cancer, it's difficult to participate in the actual conversation – the one taking place in the room. I feel ashamed. So many people get sick. And still I have the unerring sense that my disease is deserving of constant discussion.

—

At other moments I am engulfed by despair of the worst kind, the kind that is characterised by a lack of words, a despair that you can only possibly describe with the word 'despair'.

—

Once I wrote a thesis about death anxiety in the work of Heidegger and Sartre. About how, when faced with death, we finally realise that no one else can die for us, and that no one else can live for us, either, thus allowing us to break free from the conventions of the masses and lead the life that truly works for us. I thought it was a beautiful idea. Little did I know that, in reality, it is a truly horrendous thing to have to make a big life change based on a confrontation with death. But I too am changing for the better, as though enormous hands are kneading me into a new, improved form. I am becoming smoother. More focused.

—

Of course I have no idea what I'm supposed to do with this new form. When it comes down to it, I only knew I had cancer for sure for a period of one and a half weeks. Ever since, I've been guessing, hoping that in the coming years no recurrences or metastases reveal themselves. The transient nature of my period of treatment has meant that, since my operation, I've had this

31

feeling of standing here with my hands empty, and I needed to write this book in order to make time seem real, to extend the experience of my sickness. But I have no idea what to do once I've handed this manuscript over to my editor in a few days' time. How can I pick up my life again? When I know that I have ten years of uncertainty and MRI tunnels and lung scans ahead of me? When I know that I'll never be able to use my right arm the way I could before, while those enormous hands keep kneading and kneading and hurling me between endless hope and perseverance and fear and gratitude and the desire to live and the desire to never again have to get out of bed? In other words, how am I supposed to Keep Calm and Carry On?

—

My story is just one story, a story that I am slowly and cautiously coming to believe might have a positive ending. After an arduous diagnosis period, I had the luck to be operated on by a brilliant surgeon in one of the most advanced specialist hospitals in the country. With a little more luck this book might make up that chunk of my pension money I was forced to give up. But not every cancer story has a positive ending. Each year in the Netherlands forty-five thousand people die of this disease. And exactly how many people survive cancer with bodily or psychological scars, I'm not sure. And I'm not sure, either, of how many people have difficulty in taking out a mortgage or occupational disability insurance following their illness. What I do know is that the suffering of others is not something to be judged, ever, and that the right question to ask someone who is going through something difficult, whether that's illness or poverty or fleeing a war-torn country, is not 'What's in this for me?' but 'How are you feeling?'

—

And then I would feel a little foolish and needlessly melodramatic, but only a little.

Evaporate, Condensate

These are strange times, unstable times.
Seasons change, but never turn
into holidays.

You coexist with other bodies
that piss, dribble, rant, shit. All the while
a choir in a minor key softly screaming,

Your body is sick, but you will heal, this will fade.
You'll lie in the grass, stiller, thinner,
receive visitors looking fashionably underweight.
Cancer has no calendar, so be patient.

Evaporate, condensate. Even disasters
are composites of events, not products of fate.
You just have to distil, then ablate:
You will heal. This will fade.

Tomorrow Will Last
Twenty-Four Hours

Those twenty-four hours belong entirely to you

✦ ✦ ✦ ✦ ✦

Poëzie

Op het moment voelt het wel
een beetje alsof ik weer achter het
zwembadgebouw een verstopplaats
loop te zoeken ja, een vochtige plek
met plastic frietbakjes
en bladgroen voor mijn ogen.
Ver weg knaagt iets
een weg in mij, wat veiligheid
zou kunnen zijn, maar zo
voel ik me eigenlijk altijd
wel een beetje als ik net
ben klaargekomen
en alleen nog maar het muffe dons
van de dekens ruik. Ik probeerde
de hele dag op het woord
'Bastognekoeken' te komen
en toen dat eindelijk lukte,
bleef ik gewoon op bed zitten. Poëzie
lijkt me vandaag een land
waar ik geen ticket naar toe
heb gekregen, een oude geliefde
van wie ik het nummer
nog niet uit mijn telefoon
durf te wissen, een ver eiland
vol pinguïns.

L.M.
5 June 2013

Poetry

At the moment it feels a bit like
those times I would try to find
a hiding place behind
the gym building yep, a dank place
with views of chip packets
and chlorophyll.
From far away something
gnaws at me, it could be
a lost sense of safety or something, but
really that's how I always feel
as if I've just cum
and now all I can do is smell
the mildew on the sheets. I tried
the whole day to remember
the name of this particular
brand of biscuits
and when it finally happened I didn't move
from the bed. Poetry
today seems to me like a place
I've not been given a ticket to, an old love
whose number I still can't
bring myself to delete, a distant island
populated by penguins.

S.C.
9 November 2016

Translator's Note: Dear Lieke

Dear Lieke,

The last time I saw you we began the evening in Café de Jaren on Nieuwe Doelenstraat, Amsterdam, a spacious canalside bar frequented by arty types and students from the nearby university buildings. We were talking intently. A man walked up to our table and pointed a finger at the book I'd just given you. It was a copy of my own then recent poetry collection. You picked up the book and began selling it to the interloper in the style of a telemarketer or door-to-door salesperson, which was at once dismissive and eminently charming, and as I watched you perform for me and this stranger I thought consciously of how much I like you. The man – somewhat bewildered – soon left us alone again, at which point, wanting a cigarette to follow the wine I'd just finished, I asked if you were smoking (we'd smoked together before) and you said no, because you had cancer, and I felt embarrassed, having not wanted to assume anything of the fact of your diagnosis. Later that evening, at a literary event where I had just read a piece on the subject of shame, you asked me if I felt that I was a particularly shameful person, which seemed to be a question concerning my capacity for feelings of shame (rather than an implied judgement), and I didn't quite know how to respond.

Dear Lieke,

In some ways, I have no shame; at other times, I am overpowered by it. Translation is a bit like this: one moment you might feel entitled to, or at least in tune with, the source material, while at other times you find yourself immobilised by the dreaded imposter syndrome that creeps in every time you attempt to engage with the other's work in the other('s) language. I related this feeling to some of my girlfriends who translate, and they nodded solemnly in concurrence. This common experience suggests that the work of translation is frequently inhibited by feelings of shame, and it got me thinking about translation's relationship to shame, about how the translation dynamic corresponds to, or perhaps reinforces, the mechanisms through which the shame affect functions.

Dear Lieke,

As we both know, shame manifests when a person perceives a discrepancy between a projected standard of how they believe they should be – how they *could* have been – and how they see themselves as being in actuality. So, in instances of shame, there's the real, actual self plus two imagined selves: one who made the right decisions, who is endlessly humane to both herself and others; and another who is irrevocably flawed, scarred, with those flaws permanently on the verge of exposure.

Similarly, translation is a three-way street, in the sense that the translation process always involves an author (and her text – the source text), a translator and a translation. When we police translations by strenuously enforcing 'fidelity', we engineer shame in the translator by forcing her to measure her translation, which is an extension of herself, against an imagined or notional translation that is flawless – perfect in its equivalency.

Judged in this way, the translator will almost definitely fail in her task, just as vulnerable humans fail when they measure themselves against imagined, idealised and non-existent selves. Because equivalence between languages simply doesn't exist in the way we would like to think it does (theorists like Kwame Anthony Appiah have shown this time and time again). On the other hand, if we do away with 'fidelity', adopting instead some other kind of value system, the translator might be released from the pressure of a projected standard that is ultimately a shame-inducing illusion.

Dear Lieke,

I am ashamed when I find myself thinking about this book –
your book – in terms of the effect that it is having on me, on
my self. I have always experienced a degree of health anxiety,
and so translating a manuscript, albeit short, that is not only
about cancer, but that is written largely in the first person and
the present tense, awakens certain latent, obsessive behaviours.
To rewrite, read, revise and reread an account of the
symptoms of cancer, its diagnosis and treatment is to repeat,
unwittingly, a hypochondriac's mantra. The effect of this, for
me, has been a return to the fever dream of online symptom
searches, followed by a flurry of visits to my GP. But every
time a test would come back clear, my focus would simply
shift to another part of my body, where muscle spasms/
new pain/unusual discharge/discolouration/etc. suggested
underlying causes that I found myself unable to ignore.

This renewed hypochondria was exacerbated by an article
I read in the *New Yorker* on the medical gaze and gendered
perceptions of pain (the article advises women to bring 'a
sensible-seeming man' along to medical appointments – 'it's
the best way to ensure that you are given the benefit of the
doubt'). At the time of reading, I had just learnt of a friend
of a friend who, turned away repeatedly from her doctors'
surgery where her GP had forced her to downgrade the
pain she was experiencing on a numerical scale, paid for a
private diagnosis in order to prevent her own death by burst
appendix. And I had our meeting in Café de Jaren fresh
in mind too, when you told me that you were certain that
not only your age but your gender had had an impact on
the way you were perceived and treated by the two physios,
three replacement physios, GP, orthopaedist, radiologist and
neurologist who failed you in ways big and small the first time
round.

I do my best to derail my paranoid responses during
and after the translation process, to avoid projecting my own

selfish fears onto your narrative, but I also try to remind myself that pain is not always psychosomatic, and that, just as importantly, the notion of a non-egotistical response to a text – whether I'm tasked with its translation or not – is itself a projected standard, an illusion.

P.S. I have been reading *The Cancer Journals* to better understand your work. In Lorde's words: 'fear and anxiety are not the same at all. One is an appropriate response to a real situation which I can accept and learn to work through … But the other, anxiety, is an immobilising yield to things that go bump in the night, a surrender to namelessness, formlessness, voicelessness and silence.' How can I tell one from the other?

Dear Lieke,

How can you – that's me, you, 'one', anyone – be expected to read and internalise literature without forming an egotistical – that is, a subjective – response? This is precisely where so-called 'equivalency' or 'faithfulness' in translation fall down. Translators can never ever be neutral in the way they're so often thought to be.

When we published 'Poetry', my translation of your 'Poëzie', online, along with a few other pieces, I immediately started receiving Twitter notifications for comments that said things like 'in the Dutch poem there's a "swimming pool building", not a "gym building"' and '"klaargekomen" translates as "to come" – "cum" sounds much harsher'. They were corrections of my translation by (uniquely, but not accidentally) men who believed in equivalency and who had looked straight past the possibility – no, the probability – that we had been working together on these translations for several weeks, if not longer, that we had made decisions based on the particularities of the English, on its effect. More than that, though, these were men who felt – no, who feel – that they somehow *own* language. And that the women dealing in the language that they own owe them some form of rent on it. Some land tax. My initial reaction to such admonishments was one of shame. I had been found out, and I felt like an imposter again, until you, Lieke, told those men directly that you hadn't wanted me to be 'faithful' to your poems if it meant limiting the translated texts, that you had wanted me to have freedom in the process, that you admired my writing and thinking on translation. Indeed, in the note that accompanied the publication of those poems, I had proposed my alternative to 'fidelity', which is 'intimacy', and in an email you told me that you liked what I had written, that you valued my ideas. My ego felt soothed, welcomed, once again, into the space of the translation, with the imposter conjured by my creepy superego temporarily pushed aside.

Dear Lieke,

Who do I think I am? This was the question asked by writer and translator Kate Briggs at a lecture I attended in Glasgow yesterday afternoon, and it's the question I ask of myself now, after rereading what I've written concerning my response to translating your work and acknowledging the space that I am proposing to take up in the Pavilion book via these letters. Kate has translated Roland Barthes, and yesterday she spoke so honestly about the imposter syndrome this has inevitably engendered in her, about how she attempts to harness the energy of shame and embarrassment in translation to make something valuable. In her case, this something valuable was, in addition to her translations themselves, her book *on* translation, *This Little Art*, as well as, of course, the very lecture I was watching her give, in which she explored the question of literary (self-)identification through Linda Alcoff's 'The Problem of Speaking for Others'. I suppose it must be the case that I am similarly harnessing my shame by writing this text to you and your book's prospective readers.

Dear Lieke,

There are – unquestionably – things about my translation of 'Poëzie' that I would now change, only they are not the so-called 'errors' highlighted by our landlords, but more fundamental things concerning my interpretation of your text, things that have shifted as my perspective has shifted over the course of the past three years. (Who would I be if this wasn't the case?)

I am in no way arguing against the expertise of the translator; at least for now, I firmly believe that the translator ought to share an intimacy not only with the source text author, but with the source language and culture (the term 'bridge translation' is anathema to me). But a translator is, after all, only ever a reader – hopefully, if she is translating your work, she will be your *best* reader, by which I mean someone who understands your work and its context, and, above all, who has time to not only translate, but to rewrite your work in the target language (the language being translated into). But she will nonetheless be a person who is fixed in a particular moment, in a particular place and time. She will never, ever be a neutral entity. She is human. And she will make mistakes; she will have her whims.

Dear Lieke,

Why 'intimacy'? As a proposal for a new ideal in translation, 'intimacy' began with the observation that, while 'fidelity' implies the presence of a primary source of power, 'intimacy' indicates a mutual, consensual and willing exchange between two or more subjects without referencing (an) authority at all. And so intimacy is about developing a sincere engagement with the source text, author and culture, about 'getting close'. To quote Gayatri Chakravorty Spivak, 'It's not just destruction. It's also construction. It's critical intimacy, not critical distance. So you actually speak from inside.'

This seemed a particularly fitting model for your work, Lieke, because there is a deep intimacy in the way *you* seek to connect with *your* audience. I perceive it in the amount of credit you give your readers when you switch quickly between a voice of dry sarcasm and a more earnest one, trusting that those who engage with your work will recognise the difference.

Dear Lieke,

There is so much that I admire in your writing, which is in many ways different to my own. We met most recently, the weekend before last, at De Ysbreeker at Weesperzijde 23, which, being a little outside of Amsterdam's main centre, was more bougie brunch territory than De Jaren. We were talking about hair colour (I'd never realised that you in fact dye yours), and, laughing, you showed me, on your phone, an article from 2006, which featured a photo of you with your natural, mousey brown. It was an interview with you when you were still at high school and had won some poetry competition, and you drew my attention to the part where you are quoted as having said, 'Wat ik wel kan zeggen, is dat ik toegankelijke poëzie niet bevredigend genoeg meer vind', meaning, in my own, quick translation, 'What I can say is that I no longer find accessible poetry enough'. You smiled wryly as you noted that now, over ten years later, and with several books and degrees to your name, you hold more or less the inverse opinion.

Your poetry is accessible and smart at the same time, Lieke, and that is just one of the things I admire about your way of working and your ambitions for your writing. Conveying your sense of openness in the English has been important to me and it's something that has been threatened, to some extent, by the disparity between Dutch and English humour (both sarcastic, but the Dutch considerably drier, from where I'm standing), and by the regular, Netherlands-specific cultural references dotted throughout the manuscript you sent me a few months ago. On that point, I am sure that the inclusion of Dutch brands and place names – Croky, Praxis, Xenos, Twente, Tilburg – will all be questioned. I am sure that I will get another slew of comments along the lines of '"meester" means "headmaster" not "judge"'. But I am also sure that your UK readers will find their own ways to understand and voice these Dutch words, and I have faith that we are in a time where the confrontation with 'foreign' terms and an unfamiliar political system will warrant interest rather than Anglophone arrogance.

Dear Lieke,

I could continue for a long time writing these letters, these tiny dispatches containing thoughts on our friendship, this translation, on translation in general. I am sure that my continuing to write them is in part a conceit I have adopted in order not to have to relinquish this manuscript, which I feel I could read, revise and reread indefinitely. But we're getting – quite rightly – some pressure from Pavilion now, who have been endlessly patient since the original translation we were working on came to a brief halt, back in March, when you were at long last correctly diagnosed.

I was Holland at the time, and we had been due to meet the following day. You emailed me, saying that you had to postpone. You gave me the news. I remember walking down the road near my parents' house, in Bergen, afterwards, talking on the phone to another friend, back in England. I was deeply shocked and upset. I was also somewhat ashamed of my reaction. *Who am I to cry about this?* I was thinking and asking. How well did I really know you? Was this emotional reaction a kind of *speaking for* that I was uncomfortable with because of the sense of affective appropriation it gave off?

This is a question for another essay. I'm going to stop deferring and send this to you and to the press. We've translated this book quickly and with a harried excitement, and I'm signing off now with a sense of anticipation at seeing your book take on a new life in the English and with utter gratitude for your generosity in the translation process.

Thank you, Lieke.

Sophie

Notes and Acknowledgments

Many thanks to my family, friends, everyone at Uitgeverij Pluim, Pavilion Poetry and Tilt, and to all the medical staff at the oncology and orthopaedic departments of the AMC. And to Simone.

The poem 'Treats' was commissioned by the Rotterdam Arts and Sciences Lab. The RASL is a collaborative platform of the Erasmus University Rotterdam, Codarts University for the Arts and the Willem de Kooning Academy that seeks to bring together art and science in education and research.

The final lines of 'Treats' are an appropriation of a philosophical proposition from Ludwig Wittgenstein's *Tractatus Logico-Philosophicus* (1921), commonly shortened to *Tractatus*; *Investigations* is the shortened title for his posthumously published *Philosophical Investigations* (1953).

For those who want to know more about how the pharmaceutical industry makes profit out of the suffering of cancer patients, see, for example, Mariana Mazzucato's 'Big Pharma is hurting drug innovation', as published in the *Washington Post*: www.washingtonpost.com/news/theworldpost/wp/2018/10/17/pharmaceutical. In this piece Mazzucato cites a Goldman Sachs analyst who asked, while making forecasts for the biotech and pharmaceutical sector, 'Is curing patients a sustainable business model?'

The two main texts cited in 'How Are You Feeling?' are Audre Lorde's *The Cancer Journals* (London; San Francisco: Sheba Feminist Publishers, 1985) and Susan Sontag's *Illness as Metaphor and AIDS and Its Metaphors* (London: Penguin, 2002).

The poem 'Evaporate, Condensate' was written for the project

A History of the Dutch Sonnet on www.neerlandistiek.nl under the editorial guidance of Marc van Oostendorp.

The *New Yorker* article mentioned in Sophie's translator's note is 'Memoirs of Disease and Disbelief' by Lidija Haas, which can be read in full here: www.newyorker.com/magazine/2018/06/04/memoirs-of-disease-and-disbelief. Kate Briggs's *This Little Art* is published by Fitzcarraldo Editions. The quote from Gayatri Chakravorty Spivak comes from an interview in the *Los Angeles Review of Books*: lareviewofbooks.org/article/critical-intimacy-interview-gayatri-chakravorty-spivak.

Thank you, Sophie, for being an amazing translator and friend.